T H

WALLC267

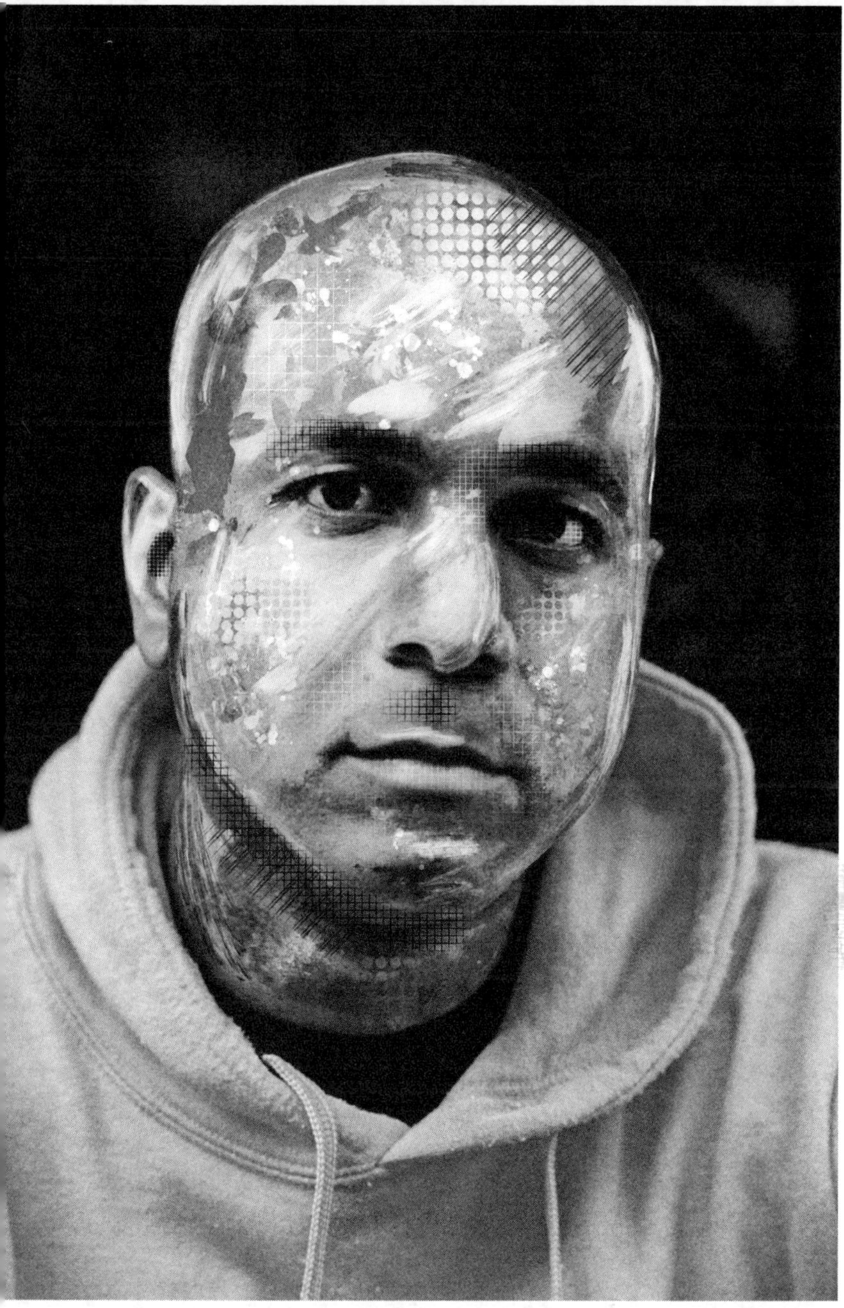

THE MIND OF WALLO267

For more information:

@wallo267:

Bookwallo267@gmail.com // Wallo267.com

Cover design: @devkamera
Cover photo: @philmeyer__
Layout design: Jessica Angerstein
ISBN: 978-1-64687-034-9

Printed in the United States of America

To my big brother Lil Steve—
Thank you for motivating me
to where I am & where I'm going!

MISS & LOVE YOU!

Contents

Intro ... 1
Throw It Away ... 3
Shortcuts Lead To Dead Ends ... 5
You Can't Have One Move In The Paint ... 7
Don't Judge That Young Bul ... 9
Believe In Yourself at the Bottom ... 11
Ego Is Killing Us ... 13
Move to Lock In Your Next Move ... 15
Stop Bullshittin ... 17
Clean Your Heart ... 19
Finished Product ... 21
You Don't Really Want It ... 23
Who Do You Be With? ... 25
Check Your Homies ... 27
I Share My Story Every Day ... 29
Show Up ... 31
Play All Four Quarters ... 33
Listen, Little Brother ... 35
Step Back/Up. De/Re-Program ... 37
Stop Waiting and Start Working ... 39
Go Get Your Dream ... 41

Open That Cell 43
Assess Liability 45
Stop Hating on Yourself 47
You Got the Same Shot 49
"Happy" Belong to You 51
Do You Really Want to Win? 53
Let Them Be 55
The Follow Up 57
It's Cool If You Don't Know. 59
Be the Ocean, Not the Wave 61
The Look Will Kill You 63
Remember that Moment 65
Accountability/ Self Discovery 67
Get It Out of Your Mind 69
Pimped by Future Perception. 71
Convince Yourself That You Can 73
Alright, but Not Better 75
Anger Will Age You 77
Don't Compete With Me, Eat With Me 79
Your Future Is Brighter 81
It's Not About Who Likes It 83
Know Your Rooms 85
Grind Activates Shine 87
Watch Energy, Not Words 89

Network to Create a Movement 91
I Was 4 Different People 95
When You Know Who a Person is, You Don't Have to Worry 97
Peeking and Ain't Speaking 99
Don't Fear Numbers on the Internet 101
Use Your Words Carefully 103
Delete Them Out Your Phone 105
Copy & Paste ≠ Success 107
The Bottom Dictates Culture 109
Divorce the Lie 111
When the Plate Get Bigger the Hate Get Bigger 113
You Can Accept Praise but Can You Accept Being Checked? 115
Your Real Life Vs. Their Fake Life 117
Your Dreams Belong to You 119
The Receipt Holders 121
Your Grind is Everything 123
Everything You Need is Here 125
Challenge Yourself 127
Affiliation Will Will Your Situation 129
Brains & Bread 131
Fix Your F#%King Clock! 133
Get Out Of Your World 135
Overthinking Killed Your Plan 137

Fake Has Us All Traumatized & Confused 139
Follow After You 141
The Corner 143
Don't Do Popular, Do You 145
When You're On or When You're Gone 147
The Blame Game 149
Burnt Out 151
Experience Is Your Best Friend 153
It's Never Too Late 155
From the Inside Out 157
Get Away From Yes People 159
Listen While You're Winning 161
Don't Beef with Information 163
Kill That Entitlement 165
Love Loves Love 167
Look at What You Got 168
I Prayed for My Enemies 169
Straighten Out Yesterday 171
Push Through! 173

INTRO

My father disappeared a month before I turned 2 years old. In the 80s, I would take weekly trips to see my stepfather in prison. A week after my 11th birthday I got arrested for armed robbery. A week later, I got arrested again. On September 19, 1990 I got sent away to a juvenile facility for a year. I came home and got arrested again—ROBBERY! I went on to spend 5 years in the juvenile system. By the time I was 17 I was sitting in prison, charged as an adult, sentenced to 6½ to 25 years and then I got an additional 13½ to 27 years (2 armed robberies and 2 firearm violations). In 1998, I was cellmates with my stepfather Big Hip (RIP) who I used to visit in the 80s at the same prison. In 2005, I was cellmates with my brother Lil Steve. I get off parole October 29, 2048. But no matter what, I'll never let yesterday's losses stop me from connecting with tomorrow's wins!

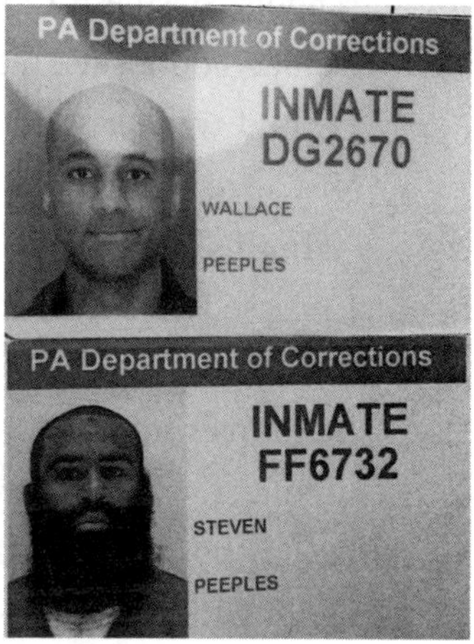

Since I walked out of prison on February 18, 2017, accountability has been my best friend and rejecting excuses is my hobby! Now I'm a paid speaker, social connector & disruptor, co-host of the *Million Dollaz Worth of Game* podcast (weekly #1 Apple Music podcast, Barstool Sports network) and host of *Where's WALLO267* (interviewing athletes, entertainers & entrepreneurs, etc.). I did a TED Talk ('I forgave my brother's killer'), been featured on the NFL network, spoke at universities, schools, business functions, hosted events for Reebok, Puma, Footlocker, etc. I also released a motivational EP and was featured on Daymond John's (*Shark Tank*) Visualize album.

In this book you'll find some of my favorite videos that I released on social media, transcribed on paper! I don't know a lot, but I often share what I do! It's a feeling in me that forces me to let out my thoughts on life in a rather unique way. I didn't create this for everyone on the planet, it's for those whose alarm clock recently went off and are looking for an unorthodox push.

Live everyday like it's your last day on earth so when your expiration date arrives no regrets will be attached to you!

Respect & Love,

WALLO267

3.8.2017

THROW IT AWAY

Today, we're gonna throw some things away—c'mon. Come right along with me. It's a lot of things in our life that we keep holding on. That's holding us back from receiving the new 'cause it's holding us back from receiving the future. That's holding us back from receiving the good. When this thing stops, I'm gonna throw away some things personally that I got. Some things that I've been dealing with. Whether old hurt or old pain—I'm getting rid of it. And today you can get rid of it too—no matter. Go into that waste basket, somewhere that's in your life, and dump everything. Throw it into that basket. Just like you throw things and you delete it and you throw it into your phone—throw all of that old stuff that you don't need that's holding you back from receiving tomorrow—get rid of it.

And it's just like that!

8.7.2017

SHORTCUTS LEAD TO DEAD ENDS

We gonna get straight to the point with this.

Ya know—everybody—you wanna do this and do that, you wanna take a shortcut, LET ME TELL YOU SOMETHING! Shortcuts lead to dead ends! Smart cuts lead to wins! You better take the smart cuts! We gotta stop taking these shortcuts in life thinking we gonna get—you not gonna reach your destination taking no shortcut. Do what you need to do, in order to get what you need to get, in order to go where you need to go. That's what it's about. Them shortcuts—listen man, them shortcuts—I'd done been to so many dead ends… Me and my associates—we been to so many dead ends and we never met the wins. You know why?! 'Cause we took them shortcuts. That's why you gotta take them *smart cuts.* Them cuts, *"no no I'm gonna go down this block"*—no I'm gonna take this way because this is the right way to go in life. That's what you gotta do. When you're doing your business thing, you can't be: *"oh i'm just gonna, I don't wanna pay taxes, I don't wanna,"* Nooo, Nooo! Shortcuts are not gonna work. Shortcuts lead to dead ends. You hear me?! Shortcuts lead to them dead ends that you don't need to be going at—it leads to them ***dead ends***. Smart cuts lead to wins. And it's just... like... ***THAT!***

8.25.2017

YOU CAN'T HAVE ONE MOVE IN THE PAINT

You can't have one—you hear me?! You can't have one move in the paint! You can't have one move in the paint! Where you go?! If the defendant dribble you gotta know how to move around that. I'm talking about being adaptable. I'm talking about in life. I'm talking about knowing how to reinvent yourself, when the time comes. That's what the game is about. 'Cause you going just one way—alright listen—alright you're going down a track, but what happens if an accident happens? When that accident happens you gotta know how to move around it. You can't have one move in the paint! You gotta know how to operate like this: ok the culture's going this way—yeah, I am the culture, so I'm gonna go this way with it.

I know how to get myself *in there.* You gotta know how to get yourself in there, that one move is gonna kill you! ‘Cause you know why? Now I know how you’re coming! I know how you’re coming so I’mma take the ball from you every time. You can’t have one move in the paint! What’re your other moves? You gotta have multiple moves. If you’re in business you have to have multiple revenue streams. You gotta tap over here, tap over there, tap over there. You gotta have your game right. Yeah! Cause when I’m coming down there you’re always thinking I’m going that way—naw I’m gonna spin this way with the ball. Yeah, you can’t have one move in the paint. And it’s just like that!

8.27.2017

Don't Judge That Young Bul

Don't judge that young bul. *Don't judge that young bul.* You ever seen your mom get high in front of you? You ever seen your mom turn a trick in front of you? Is your pop in the penitentiary through a thousand years and you never seen him? Did your pop just run off and never was there for you? Did you uncle or your aunt molest you as a kid? Well then—don't judge that young bul. A lot of these youngins suffer from post-traumatic stress disorder. They've been exposed to things that a kid ain't supposed to be exposed to and you wonder why they're wilding out. You wonder why they're walking around bucked up. You know why? Hurt people hurt people. And sometimes hurt people cry out for help in different ways. But don't judge that young bul if you ain't been through what he been through. You don't even know what he been through, but you keep judging, talking about they animals and they need to be this, that, and the third... Don't judge that young bul, unless you walked in *his* shoes, unless you went through *his* pain. If you don't understand that—c'mon man. And if you ain't trying to add then be quiet. All that you trying to be scared of him—you supposed to be from the community—you need to dig yourself. But don't judge that young bul. Because hurt people hurt people and they're hurting and crying out for help. And it's just like that!

9.10.2017

Believe In Yourself at the Bottom

You gotta believe in yourself at the bottom, you hear me? I'm talking about when you're at the bottom. When I was in prison, I wouldn't have a dime on my books, I wouldn't have no food in my cabinets. I ain't have nothing, but you know what?! I'd be walking that track, talking that smack.

"Yeah man, I'm going out there and making it happen! I'mma buy my mom a house, I'mma do this for my grandma, I'mma do this for my nieces and nephews. I'm gon' do this, I'm gon' do that, I'm gon' do this, I'm gon' do that."

At the end of the conversation I'd say, "Yo man, when we get in the block, let me get two soups."

"Man you were just talking about you gonna do this, that, and the third!"

"I ain't telling you what I got, I'm telling you what I'mma get—goddaaamn baby, c'mon man!"

Noone ain't supposed to know I'm that guy! I'm that guy in them shackles. I'm that guy at the ground. I'm that guy when I fell. I'm that guy when I lose. I ain't gon' stop being who I am! You kidding me?! I'mma believe in myself at the bottom no matter what, no matter the situation. You better believe in yourself at the bottom. Believe in yourself wholeheartedly. Don't even worry about what nobody else is doing. You better believe in you. It ain't about what you got now, it's about what you gon' get. It ain't about what you ain't making now, it's about what you gon' make happen. And that's how I do it—I believe in myself at the bottom, and it's JUST. LIKE. ***THAT!***

2.14.2018

Ego Is Killing Us

Ego is killing us! Ego is killing us!

Relationships, friendships, family members—IT'S KILLING US! We can't let it go! Because if I let go of my ego and I compromise, that means that I admit that I was wrong. That means you're right—you win, I lose. Ego is killing us! It's killing relationships, it's killing friendships because our ego is superseding everything. It's superseding the times that we got in. It's superseding the hard moments that we got through together. And it's superseding the love, the love that we say we got for each other—it's superseding that. Ego is killing us. We gotta stay focused here. We gotta figure out—how can we do this. How can we say: you know I'm gonna make the sacrifice and I'mma let go of my ego and admit that I'm wrong so that we can grow together. That's what I'mma do. So we can grow. So that we can move on and we can learn from this journey that we've been through. We can learn from this down moment that we had. But EGO IS KILLING US! Nobody wants to admit it. And it's JUST LIKE… ***THAT!***

2.17.2018

Move to Lock In Your Next Move

You gotta move to lock in your next move. You hear me? You gotta move to lock in your next move!

When I was in prison, I was working for 19 cents (an hour). But I was working for 19 cents like it was worth 42 cents. When I got to 42 cents, I was working like I was worth a pay raise that didn't even exist! Your WORK gotta represent your WORTH. And once your work represents your worth, people are gonna pay you your worth. But you gotta be willing to put it in. You can't be in a position saying, *"Oh no, I'm cool..."* No, don't lax nothing! Secure your future with the moves right now! Every move that I make you looking at me like, *"Damn, Wallo don't stop,"* naww—I overperform! I'm locking in my future, right now!

Lock in your future right now—you hear me?! Let your worth equal your work, and let your work equal your worth, but you gotta put it in every day. And you gotta work. I'm telling you when I had that 19 cents I was like, "Ahh man!" I gave them a dollar worth of work and it wasn't even a dollar pay raise that existed! Move to lock in your next move. And it's just like THAT!

2.17.2018

Stop Bullshittin

When you gon' stop bullshittin, huh? When you gon' stop bullshittin? You got all the plans. You keep talking about the plans. You keep telling everybody what you about to do. Time been going by and you ain't do shit yet. When you gonna stop bullshittin?? You know the relationship is bullshit—why you ain't cut it off yet? You got all the ammunition in you—why you ain't pull the trigger yet, huh?! When you gon' stop bullshittin?! Everybody keep playing: *"Oh yeah you gonna be... oh yeah it's gonna be..."*

Ehh! C'mon man—KILL THAT!! MOVE OUT!! EXECUTE!! Stop talking! You keep rapping all the time! STOP BULLSHITTIN!! That's the problem: everybody keeps pacifying you, *"Yeah it's gonna be good... yeah it's gonna be..."* Yeah, yeah, yeah, yeah yeah—when you gon' pull the trigger?! Everything—you got all this stuff you need to let go of in life. You got all these people you need to let go of in your life. You got all these things you need to move out on and you ain't do nothing yet—you just still keep rapping.

STOP BULLSHITTIN!!

And it's just. Like… *That!*

2.19.2018

Clean Your Heart

Clean your heart. You keep wondering, *"Damn why this ain't..."* Naw, naw—before you get to the next levels of life, you gotta be willing to cleanse your heart. You gotta clean your heart! All that anger, all that bitterness, all that resentment, all that hurt. All those things you're going through, you gotta keep focused on that. That's why you can't do what you need to do. You gotta clean your heart! Who you're angry with, who you're mad with. Who brings envy in your heart... you gotta let that go—you hear me? You gotta cleanse your heart. Once you clean your heart so many things will come in. Because if your heart ain't right, things are just not gonna happen for you. You gots to clean your heart! Cleanse your heart! C'mon man. Listen—stop playing with yourself. Cause things are not gonna happen for you, because you're not approaching life in a pure manner. You're not approaching life in a proper manner, it's not gonna happen. You gotta clean your heart and I guarantee you things are gonna change for you. Your world gonna open up, but you gotta clean your heart. And it's just LIKE ***THAT!***

2.24.2018

Finished Product

No, no, no, no. That ain't how the game work. That ain't how the game work. I understand that you're in love with the finished product, but let me tell you something: you know it was a journey attached to that. It was a journey. It was a struggle attached to that. But you're sitting there, you're thinking, *"Ohh man this is beautiful! This is what I want for myself. This is what I wanna do. I wanna be at the party—I wanna be at the celebration!"* But the celebration is celebrating overcoming that struggle that it went through at the beginning.

I remember back in the day, uhh, '90s/ mid '90s, I went to a concert. You know who was there? Jay-Z. And you know what? He wasn't on the top—he wasn't top-billing, he was just on the show. He was featured on somebody that was featured on the show. He did one verse for Original

Flavor—'Can I Get Open?' Now he's where he's at now. But it was a journey then. It was the chitlin circuits when he was doing those small clubs. Before he got to where he's at.

Listen—you can be in love with the finished product, but you gotta embrace the journey that came with it. And it's just. Like. ***THAT!***

2.24.2018

You Don't Really Want It

C'mon man! You keep playing games. You keep talking. You keep burning your friends out. YOU DON'T REALLY WANT IT! You got everything you need in order to make it happen. Every place that you're trying to go, you got all the tools you need. You got the people that's gonna help you, you got the robots that's gonna help you, but you ain't doing nothing. You just keep talking—lip service. *"I wanna do this, I wanna go here, I wanna go..."* YOU DON'T REALLY WANT IT! If you want it you gon' make it happen. You gon' connect with the people that can introduce you to the places that you're trying to be at. You gon' connect with these robots and find you all the information that you need in order to connect with the places and the things you're trying to do in life. But you ain't doing it. You just keep talking. You just keep rapping. *"I wanna do this.... I wanna go... Why this?... Oh they hating on me..."* AIN'T NOBODY PAYING YOU ATTENTION! Stop thinking everybody's paying you attention. What makes you so important that people don't want you to win? Think about that. You don't really want it. You don't really want to win. And it's JUST LIKE... ***THAT!***

2.25.2018

Who Do You Be With?

Surround yourself with only people that can lift you higher. That's what Oprah Winfrey once said.

Think about it—who do you be with? I used to be with the guys that were on their way to prison, that were on their way to the graveyard, that were on their way to failure. That's who I used to be with, so you know what? I went to prison, I was a failure. That's where I was at. But think about it—do you be with the people that win? Do you be with the people that wanna educate themselves and become a better person then they were yesterday, or do you be with the people that only wanna gossip, that only wanna hate, that only wanna envy what everybody else got going on, because they don't got nothing going on their-self. Because whoever you be with, that's a representation of who you are. Don't try to say, *"Oh no, they be like that..."*—naw—if you be around people that gossip every day, you're a gossiper! You know what you are? Because you're enabling that, you're empowering that—that's what you're about. If you be around winners, you're a winner. And it's JUST. LIKE. ***THAT!***

2.25.2018

Check Your Homies

You gotta stop playing, you hear me? You gotta stop playing. We gotta start checking our homies. You gotta check your homie. Your homie in the club, he poppin' bottles, he doing this, he buying *this*, he buying this, but he ain't taking care of his kids. He ain't taking care of his responsibility at home, but you out here doing this. When you don't check him, you know what you're doing? You're cosigning and saying that that's cool. C'mon man! We gotta do better. Like Rich Dollarz said: You gotta check your homies. You doing *this* and you doing this... *NAW*—take care of your babies. You spending all this money. How you spending all this money and your daughter ain't right, your son ain't right? C'mon man—think about that, man. We gotta start checking each other. That's the problem. We never wanna deal with the real facts or we wanna be cool. *"Oh that ain't my business"*. Yeah it is your business 'cause if he with you, that's a reflection of you, and you cosigning that nut stuff. You gotta check your homies, you hear that? Start checking your homies. ***And it's just like that!***

2.27.2018

I Share My Story Every Day

Everybody that's taking this journey with me, I just want to thank you. When I was a teenager I was married to the streets of Philadelphia and I never thought that I would see this day. I never thought that I would be around these type of days.

Most of my homeboys—they died in their teenage years. They never made it to be 20. I made it for a reason—I'm here. I'm here to tell my story. I'm here to tell the journey of my homies that ain't make it. My friends that ain't make it. *I'm here.* So, I tell my story every day. I give you the information that I went through. All the pain and all the things that I went through I try to share it with everybody. I share my story. If you got a story out there that can help somebody else, share it, ya know. It's not hard—just share it. 'Cause you don't know how your story could help somebody else.

So I'm here for a reason. I didn't get killed out there. A lot of my homies died and I didn't go with them. I didn't get life in prison—I didn't kill nobody, but I was a thief. I was a liar. I was a cheater. I was a felon—whatever you want me to be. But I went through all of that so I could tell you my story. And I hope that you can learn from my story and don't live my story. For all you youngins out there.

3.4.2018

Show Up

C'mon—no, no, no, no, no, no! You gotta show up, you hear me? You gotta show up! I done showed up for you! I done showed up for everybody. It didn't matter if I was broke, I didn't have nothing to wear—I had to wear the same thing. If I was sick—I didn't care what was going on. I was emotional because something had happened to my family or whatever. I had to show up! Because I said this is what I do! If you don't do what you say you do, then you don't do it!

You gotta show up! We keep saying, *"Oh no, I ain't gon' come..."* It's people I be looking for—I done seen and I done been following; I've been into their products, whatever they got going on and then I come through. They're not there no more. I'm like what happened?! They done gave up because it got hard. Listen: it's gonna get hard. So what?! But you gotta go through that. You gotta go through all that. And you gotta show up when it gets hard. I'm telling you, that's what I done—that's why I'm here. I'm here every day. You ever see me take—I don't take no days off! I'm never gon' take no days off! Because you never know the day you take off—you need to show up, because the people was there for you. The people were there to take you to another level, but you gotta show up! No matter what happens! I'mma show up every day! You better show up every day because your moment is coming. Your time is coming, but you gotta show up and it's Just... Like... ***THAT!***

3.6.2018

Play All Four Quarters

When you gonna play four quarters, huh?! You never played four quarters in your life. You always abandon your dreams. You always abandon your goals. C'mon! So what?! So what it was an interception?! So what the quarterback got sacked?! So what if it was a fumble?! You gotta make it to halftime! You don't even make it to halftime! You give up in the first quarter on everything you do! Everything you ever started, you give up! Why you keep giving up on you?! Why you keep abandoning you?! Why you keep abandoning the things you say you want?! C'mon baby—make it until the clock stops!! Play 'til the clock stops!! The game is never over for you until the clock stops! But you gotta make it through them 4 quarters! C'mon! Make it through them! You gonna go through hardships. Sometimes they gon' get the goal.

Sometimes they gon' run it back. But that's life—you gotta assemble your team. Talk to your team, encourage your team: *"C'mon baby, WE GOT IT! Don't worry about that fumble. We got it! We gon' make it happen!"* But you gotta play the whole 4 quarters. Play the whole 4 quarters, man. Stop abandoning your dreams. Stop abandoning you. And it's just like ***THAT!***

3.7.2018

Listen, Little Brother

Do me a favor. Go get your nephew. Go get your son. Go get your little brother. Go get your little cousin. Let me holla at ‘em a little bit. Now listen little brother, let me explain something to you. We come from a place where everybody do what everybody do. But little brother, you ain't everybody. Every day that you leave your house you gon' run into some temptation. But just because you run into temptation don't mean you have to bite into the apple. Just fall back and stay who you are. Because it's a lot of things that come with that temptation. I need you to use me. Please use me everywhere you want to. Because I was the same cat standing on that corner. I was the same cat in them streets. I used to see that dude walking to school every day and I used to look at him like yeah, he's a real live square. But I'mma tell you one thing—that dude that

I thought was a real live square? He ain't never have to spend a day in jail. He ain't never have to be strip searched to go see his people. He ain't have to do none of that, but *I did.* I did that. I had to do all that because I chose to bite into that temptation. Ya'mean? While everybody was being everybody else, I wanted to be everybody else instead of being me. So my whole thing is you ain't got to do that. So keep doing what you doing and stay focused, man. And don't get caught up. Don't feed into the lure, because it's a lot of pain that come with that.

3.10.2018

Step Back / Up. De / Re-Program

So you know what you do? You step back so you can step up. But when you step up, your step up is stronger. You positioning yourself better. Think about it—the regroup. Think about it—sometimes you gotta deprogram yourself in order to reprogram yourself. And when you reprogram yourself, your approach to life is stronger. You hear me? But you're saying, "*I don't wanna stop right now. I don't wanna stop in the middle of this. I don't wanna stop 'cause I got my groove.*" And you think you ain't gonna get your groove back, but no—no! When you reapproach this thing—when you approach it, and you're stronger, after you regrouped, and after you reevaluate yourself, think about this: the groove gets stronger. The groove lasts longer. Now you're really in control of what you got going on. But you're thinking about this, *"I don't wanna stop..."* No! It's not about the stop, it's about you stepping back so you can step up and when you step up you gon' step up right! And your thing gon' be right. Think about that. You gotta deprogram yourself in order to reprogram yourself. So sometimes you gotta deprogram your situation in order to reprogram your situation. And when you reprogram your situation, you're able to approach life stronger and you're ready to better position yourself. And it's just like *THAT!*

3.10.2018

Stop Waiting and Start Working

Listen man, you gotta start working and stop waiting. Who you waiting for? You ready for this? Newsflash! Ain't nobody coming to help you! Ain't nobody coming to pass you, ain't nobody coming to give you an alley-oop. Just make that happen and then everybody's gonna come. You keep worrying, *"Oh they ain't helping me. Oh he ain't helping me. Oh why they ain't helping me? Oh man, people frontin'. Aww they this and that..."* AIN'T NOBODY COMING!

Ain't nobody come for me, I just went in! I just went! When they thought I was crazy, I kept going! I had two phones, I ain't have no money. I gotta tell you this again? I ain't have no money! I didn't have no paper, I was dead pop! I was cracked like the Liberty Bell! You understand? You know what my vehicle was? My vehicle was public transportation or any homie that I seen that had a car. I was car-hopping and everything. But you know what? I wasn't waiting, I was working! Everyday!! Everyday you gotta put that work in. You keep waiting—AIN'T NO-BO-DY COMING! Once you realize that, just turn it up. And stop over-strategizing. *"I gotta make sure my plan is this..."* YOU'VE BEEN PLANNING FOR YEARS! You ain't do nothing yet. When you gon' do something? I didn't have no plan. I ain't have time to put no plan together. You think it's, *"Oh Wallo is so strategic 'cause he had all this time in jail."* Yeah, but you know what? One little thing can mess the plan up and then reality hits, then it's on. Stop waiting and start working! And it's JUST LIKE ***THAT!***

3.14.2018

Go Get Your Dream

You keep talking about you want ________. GO GET IT! Your dreams are waiting for you! They're waiting for you on the other side at the end of the tunnel! But are you willing to go through everything you gotta go through? You willing to go through this?! You willing to go through all the ups and the downs that'll come to take to materialize your dreams?! You willing to go through that?! Go through it!! GO GET YOUR DREAM! It's waiting for you! It's waiting for you with a warm embrace. But it's still a cynic sitting there like this, *"Come on—when you gonna start?"* I don't care what you're doing! I don't care how small you think it is—but that little small little step to materialize your dream may activate something in you that may have you take it to levels you never knew that were in you! You hear me?! TURN IT UP!! GO GET

YOUR DREAMS!! GO GET IT!! Stop playing. You gotta go through this though. I'mma go through this. But I'm going through it with you every day. You see me every day go through it. The ups and downs I had to go through in life in order to get to where I am now, but it's still things that I gotta go through in order to get to where I'm going! GO THROUGH IT!! And it's JUST LIKE ***THAT!***

3.18.2018

Open That Cell

Let's talk about it—I did the time 'cause I did the crime—you ain't do nothing. We talking about self-incarceration! We talking about you put yourself in prison?! Because of your fears, because of your doubts, because of other people's opinions and you can't move?! What is the matter with you?! C'mon man. The key is inside of you. Get that key inside of you and open that cell. Open that cell. Because look at you; you're paralyzed. You're paralyzed by views, you're paralyzed by doubts, you paralyzed by fear. GET OUT OF THAT CELL! Come on! You can do it. You've been sitting in this cell all this time. It's more people in the free world in prison than it is in prison. We just throw ourselves in prison because we got all these doubts, all these fears. All these people's opinions are laid on us and now we just in this cell, sitting there. When you gon' get out of prison? When you gon' make parole? Huh?! When you gon' take that key that's inside of you and open that door? That door to your fears, that door to your doubts, and just go? Come on, man. I'm waiting for you. I made parole. What's up with you? What you doing? Huh? Stop playing games. Stop being in fear. Stop worrying about other people's opinions and just move. You got this. Go get that key inside of you and open up that gate. And don't come back! ***It's JUST LIKE THAT!***

3.19.2018

Assess Liability

When you go get that new car, what do you do? You make sure that it's gonna run—you make sure you're not buying a lemon. When you go to get that new home, you make sure everything is right. When you're ready to sign that contract for a phone or whatever, you assess a liability. When you go into a bank and you ask them for some money, you know what they do? They assess a liability. Why don't you assess the liability of the people you allow into your life? Think about that. How are these people? Do they push? Do they pull? Am I going down dealing with these people? Are these people gonna add value to my life? Are they gonna devalue my life? What's gonna happen? Think about that. We let so many people run in and out of our life, but we never assess the liability of having a relationship with them, or being in love with them, or anything. We never assess that. How can this help me or how can this hurt me? Think about that. But we do it with the vehicles in our life. We do it with the contracts that we sign. We do it with the homes we get or the apartments we rent. We do it with everybody, but you know what? We don't do it with ourselves. We don't assess the liability of the people that we allow to travel through our life. Think about that. You gotta assess the liability of the people that you allow into your life. And it's just like *THAT!*

3.20.2018

Stop Hating on Yourself

It ain't never too late! It ain't never too late to be who you would have been. *"Oh, I'm too old, I ain't got it. I shh..."* C'mon—stop playing games. Stop playing games! Talking 'bout who you can't be? I'm trying to figure out; you talking about "the haters". And I always say this: "the haters" is your marketing team. Let them work. "The haters" is your marketing team—stop worrying about them. But you know what's so crazy about it? Most of y'all are y'all biggest haters. Every time that you come up with something that you wanna do in life, you jump right out, *"Unh-unh! You can't do that! You ain't gon' be able to do that—you ain't strong enough."* And you lay right back down in the bed. You talking about the haters? You the biggest hater that you got! Hater? Stop hating on yourself! Start loving yourself and start believing in yourself.

3.20.2018

You Got the Same Shot

You playing games. You better get them noises out your head. Why you creating ghosts? You always creating these ghosts that heighten your fears. You got the same shot as everybody else. Look at it. We all at the race. We all at the line, the starting point. When you wake up in the morning, you got the same shot as everybody on the planet. When that gun go off, *"BOP!!"* You got the same shot. You got a chance to win the race—I don't care if they're a millionaire. I don't care if they up, if they down—everybody got the same shot. If you're on the planet Earth and you're breathing: you got the same shot. C'mon playing games. You keep with all this noise in your head, *"wahhh, wahhhh, wahhhhh."* You better kill that. You better kill that, you hear me? You better kill that. I don't wanna hear none of that. I'm Wallo267... and you know what? I got the same shot as everybody on the planet. I don't care who you are. I don't care how much money you got. 'Cause you know what? You already know where I'm from. I'mma turn it up every day.

And it's just… like… that.

3.21.2018

"Happy" Belong to You

"Happy" belong to you. "Happy" belong to you. You hear me? Happy belong to you. Can't nobody take your happy from you. Can't nobody dictate your happy. Can't nobody steal your happy. Can't nobody destroy your happy. That's yours! You hear me? You're 'sposed to be able to dictate your happy. You 'sposed to be able to move your happy around and own your happy. Don't be letting no situation, no relationship, no materialism—don't let *nothing* control your happy. Happy is yours. That's yours. Listen: happy belongs to *you*. It's inside of *you*. It shouldn't be inside of nobody else. Shouldn't nobody else be in a position to hold onto that. That's yours! You hear me? It's your happy. If somebody try to come and take your happy, try to destroy your happy, try to move your happy around? Get 'em outta here! Happy belong to you and it's just like that!

3.21.2018

Do You Really Want to Win?

Do you really wanna win? Do you *really* wanna win? You tired of losing?! Now, you saying you want to win—make the sacrifices necessary to win. Make the changes necessary to win! You scared of all the changes that come with winning. You gotta make some changes. You gotta let some things go. You gotta let some people go. You gotta let some outlooks go in order to win. Are you ready? You can do it. I know you can win. Because I had to let go of some of those things. I've done it! And if I can do it, you can do it. If you can see it, you can be it.

But let me tell you something—when you talk about winning? When you're talking about winning and being a winner there's a lot of things in life you gotta let go.

There's a lot of people you might have to let go. There's a lot of outlooks you might have to let go. Are you willing to let those things go to win? Ask yourself that. Ask yourself if you're really ready to win... Or if you're comfortable with being a loser? You gotta ask yourself that. But know that you can make those changes, you can make those sacrifices if it's really in your heart to be victorious at the end. To be on that podium... To be victorious.

4.1.2018

Let Them Be

You gotta let them be. Stop trying to make people something that they're not. Let them be! When they show you who they are with their actions, believe them. And that's who they are. They're not who you want them to be. I know you need somebody in your life to do this and you want somebody to do—no, that's not what they... you gotta let people do what they're good at doing. Let them be.

When I was in jail, some people would just send me pictures—I wouldn't ask them to send me money, I wouldn't ask them to come visit me. That's what they do. Some people would just write me. That's what they do.

You gotta let people be who they be and stop trying to make them who you want them to be. 'Cause that ain't the reality of it. And you gotta start respecting people's actions over their words. They are who they say they are… NO. They are what they *do*. That's the game of life! You gotta understand that and stop acting like you don't know what's up. Know what's up, man. Stop trying to make people something that they're not. And it's just like *THAT!*

4.1.2018

The Follow Up

Listen, it's about the follow up. We keep saying, *"Damn I'm trying to do this, I'm trying to do that."* Everybody that you're trying to connect with, everything that you're trying to do is in your phone. All you gotta do is follow up. See we never follow up. We'll meet somebody... we'll connect with somebody… we'll do this,... but we never follow up! Everybody you need to know, you already know!

Go in your phone. Go in your phone—check your phone. Just go through your phone and look at all the people you never reconnected with. Look at the people you never followed up with. Look at the people you never even went out to that lunch/dinner you said you were going, or that date, whatever. You never went out on them. But you know what? They're just lingering in your phone taking up space. You gots to follow up! We meet people every day that could change our lives, but we never follow up 'cause we get so consumed with all the other things that we got going on in life. We never take that time to say, "You know what? Let me go through all my connections I have. Let me go through my network of people that I done networked with in my life and during my journey." Just follow up! And I'm telling you, everything you want gon' happen. It's *just like that!*

4.2.2018

It's Cool If You Don't Know.

Stop playing games—it's cool. It's cool you don't know. 'Cause if you don't know, you can learn. But, stop acting like you know when you don't know. We keep sitting here, *"oh I don't know, I don't know,"* but you don't wanna ask nobody 'cause you got too much pride. But you can't grow if you don't know. C'mon, man! You can't glow if you don't know. C'mon man, it's cool. If you don't know, ask somebody. We keep sitting here, we'll go through and we be all, *"aww man I don't know this, I'm just gonna freestyle, but I got too much pride to ask somebody. I don't wanna ask for help."* I keep telling you help is you homie! Which it's cool if you don't know. We keep thinking that we can make it, not knowing and we can freestyle. Stop freestyling and ask somebody. Stop freestyling and acting like you know what's going on. It's cool if you don't know.

Put that pride to the side. Put that ego to the side. Put that to the side and get that game that you need. That guidance, attention, motivation and education that you need in order to take it to the next levels of life so you can grow. It's cool if you don't know. Ask somebody. And it's ***JUST LIKE THAT!***

4.2.2018

Be the Ocean, Not the Wave

Today is a funeral. It's a wave funeral. Look—you see the waves, look at all these funerals (standing on the beach, looking at the ocean with waves coming in toward the beach). The ocean never dies, though. The ocean never dies, but look at all these funerals. All these wave funerals. Don't be a wave, be the ocean. It's timeless. It's limitless. You don't have a death date when you're the ocean. But if you're a wave, here are some funerals. Look at all these funerals, all these deaths. But look at the ocean. Look. The ocean lives forever. There won't be a funeral for the ocean. And it's just like that!

4.4.2018

The Look Will Kill You

The look will kill you. You gotta watch it. Man, you be doing so much for the look that you will convince yourself that the look is really your reality. And you know what the look do? The look will kill your drive, because you done already convinced yourself that you done made it. You done convinced yourself that, *"oh I'm doing good. I got this going on."* Because of the things that you post on social media. The things that you do out there in the world, you got everybody convinced. Naw—you ain't got everybody convinced. You got *you* convinced. So you saying to yourself, *"I'm winning, I've already arrived. I made it."* That you're falling back. You ain't even trying to turn it up. You ain't even trying to take things to the next levels of life. You ain't trying to do nothing because you already said I already made it... because you really, you really, you *really* believe the lie that you created for yourself. That the lie that you created to produce and push out there to the world is real. And once you believe that, you're *done*. The look is killing you! It's all about the look, man. The look is killing you. You better kill the look, before the look kill you. And it's just... like... that!

4.7.2018

Remember that Moment

You gotta remember that moment. When them tough times come, remember that moment. That moment somewhere in your life, where it was just so rough, the world was crashing down and you were like, *"Ahhh!"* It was crashing down on you, but some way you were able to push it up off of you and you got up. You got up. That moment! We all had that moment. But you gotta remember that moment.

Right now, if you're in that rough spot, if things are hard for you, remember that moment that you felt was the hardest time *in your life*. You know what you did when that moment came, when it came crashing down on you and you said, *"Ahhh!"*?! You pushed it up! You got it up off you. You got back up and you were strong again. You gotta remember that moment.

We all had that moment. I had that moment plenty of times in my life and I got up. 'Cause we are resilient people. We're humans—we can do it! So when you go there, and if you're there right now? You in that dark place and it's hard and it's rough for you? Remember that moment and connect with that strength that you had on that day, at that moment, at that time. Remember that moment. You can get up. You can do it. And it's just like that.

4.7.2018

Accountability / Self Discovery

See, it's about self-discovery. Because we're doing this and pointing fingers and no, no—you gotta point the same finger at you. See I point my finger at me. I didn't go to jail because I just got randomly locked up, no I was really out there doing stuff. I was really out there committing crimes so when I went to prison I had to worry about—listen man, damn! I had to do that self-discovery. I had to discover what was going on inside of me to make me act a certain way or to make me do certain things. Once I did that, the game changed 'cause I took that accountability. See, that's why I ain't come home mad. That's why I didn't come home angry 'cause the girl left me or because nobody ain't send me money, or because of this person or that person. Ain't nobody tell on me, so I wasn't in a situation whereas I had to be mad at this person or that. I had to be mad at myself for putting myself in that situation, but that came about through *self discovery.* I had to discover that. That's why I'm telling you—you can sit here and think to yourself, like, *"Aww man!"* Oh no, that mad stuff—that ain't gonna get you nowhere. Be mad at yourself. Don't come home and be mad at your family. You try to be mad at everybody in the hood or be mad at the woman that chose because nobody's life stops when you go to prison. You gotta understand that. You understand people only love you when they see you, but hol' up—you went there because you went through that. But self discovery is everything: You gotta point the finger at yourself; I kept pointing the finger at myself.

4.12.2018

Get It Out of Your Mind

You better get out of slavery. You're enslaved. It ain't even back in the day and you in slavery. All the things you put in your mind of why you can't win or why you can't do this, *"Oh they racist... oh this... oh they hating..."* That's all bullshit! Make it happen! Let me tell you something: every key to every closed door on this planet is right here in your mind. All you gotta do is believe in yourself and stop BS'ing. Stop making excuses. Stop being in slavery. 'Cause every time that you say that you can't do this or can't do that because of that reason, or that reason—you're back on the plantation! You keep letting everything cripple you. C'mon man! You're extraordinary! Go out there and do what you wanna do! But first—you gotta get that stuff out of your mind. All the fears you got, all the inferiority complex, get that shit out of your mind. Go out there and get it and NEVER FORGET: the keys are right here. And it's just like *THAT!*

4.14.2018

Pimped by Future Perception.

You were ready to say something, but you didn't. You were ready to wear something, but you didn't. And the reason you didn't is because you were in fear of people's future perception of you. I'm talking about things that didn't even happen. You in the fear of future perception. *"Oh they gon's say this or do this."* Newsflash: you're being pimped. You're being pimped and you don't even dig it. You're being pimped. You're being pimped by people's perception of you, before you even—you're talking about the *future* perception of you—you're being *pimped*. You don't even dig it. They're dictating how you're gonna move. Their perception of you is dictating how you're gonna move. You're being pimped! You don't get it? Get away from them pimps. Stop being pimped and just live. Just do what you wanna do. *Live.* I live every day. I wear what I wanna wear. I say what I wanna say. I do what I wanna do. I think my own thoughts. I'm encouraging you to do that. I'm challenging you to do that. Stop being pimped and it's just like THAT!

4.15.2018

Convince Yourself That You Can

If you think you can't have it, you won't. Because as soon as you get that thought in your mind that I want this, but I'll just never be able to achieve that. I can't have that. All the ideas, all the ways, all the avenues, all the things you could do in order to get what you already convinced yourself that you can't have, 'cause you're saying to yourself, *"Aww this is too big. Oh I ain't got a degree. Oh I ain't got this, I ain't got that."* You've finessed yourself out of getting the things you really want 'cause you convinced yourself that you can't have these things. Think about that. Why do we keep convincing ourselves that we can't do certain things, that we can't be certain people, that we can't go certain places? Why do we do that? C'mon man. We gotta stop convincing ourselves. You will finesse yourself right out of a situation like, *"No, no. You ain't gon' be able to do that."* Nobody even had to do it on the outside of you. You got that in your mind and I don't understand why. Because you can do anything you want to do. You can go anywhere you want to go. You can be anything you want to be. But you know what? You gotta put the work in, in order to do that. And you gotta be able to convince yourself that you could do it, just as you convinced yourself that you can't do it. And it's just LIKE THAT!

4.17.2018

Alright, but Not Better

You can do alright, but you can't do better than me. You hear me? That's the mindset of people: you can do alright, you can be doing your thing, but you can't do better than *me.* We need to stop worrying about that. How can you say somebody else is doing better than you? C'mon! How can you put somebody above you? You shouldn't even be thinking with that mindset. You should just be focused on you. But the mindset of 'you can do alright, but you can't do better than me'—You gotta get rid of that type of thinking. You gotta get rid of that mindset. And sometimes you don't even say that to yourself—that's your attitude. That's your mindset. That's your approach. You can do alright, but you can't do better than me. C'mon that's weak stuff, man. You're supposed to be focused on what you got going on. Don't be worried about what somebody else has and stop putting people over yourself. Like I told you before, I ain't better than you and you ain't better than me. You ain't better than me and I ain't better than you. So come on with that 'you can do alright, but you can't do better than me' mindset. You ain't gotta say it, but that's your attitude. And it's just like that.

4.18.2018

Anger Will Age You

One thing that's important: anger will age you. That anger, it will age you. Think about everybody you know that's always mad, that's always miserable, that's always got bad things to say about everybody and everything. Look at them. Don't they look older than they are? Think about this: when I was in prison, people used to say to me, *"Wallo you always happy. Wallo you always laughing..."* You know why? Because it preserves you. That happiness preserves you. I knew dudes that I had by about fifteen years, had by ten years, and they were looking like they were my oldheads. You know why? That happy preserves you and that anger gon' age you! Think about it man, you gotta be like this all day (face screwed up and mad), *"ughhh, ughgh, UGHHH."* You're using too many of your muscles. When you're happy you're just light and smiling.

It's real simple, it's easy. You feel no pain. But every time your face is screwed up, you feel it, man. Anger will age you. Happiness will preserve you. And it's just like that!

4.19.2018

Don't Compete With Me, Eat With Me

Don't compete with me, eat with me. Listen, we be having family, we be having best friends, we be having associates and we will sit there and compete. Listen man, you know how to get the cars. I got the mouth-piece, I'm a people person. Don't compete with me, eat with me. We tripping—we got the game messed up. We're always thinking about competition every time somebody's ready to do something. We're never thinking about, damn—how can we come together and collaborate and make what you got going on and what I got going on stronger. Don't compete with me, eat with me!

That's what it's about. We gotta stop looking at everything like it's a competition. Like it's me against you, us against them. Naww! It's US against EVERYBODY! That's the game! When you're a family, when you're a friend, when you're an associate, when you're a colleague—that's what it's about. Don't compete with me, eat with me. Stop thinking small and start thinking big. Start thinking vast. C'mon man. A little couple dollars, no, no. It's not about getting a little bit of money, it's about getting all the money that you can as a team. Teamwork makes the dream work. Together each achieves more. Don't compete with me, eat with me. That's what it's about, man. Stop playing games. And it's just like ***that!***

4.23.2018

Your Future Is Brighter

No... no! You ain't giving up on my watch, you hear me? Your future is brighter than what you see in yourself right now. It's brighter! I remember when I got sentenced to all of that time and I go back to the holding cell. And the sheriff, he came back and said, "*Young blood, you gon' be alright, young blood. You can't see it, but it's big things coming for you. You know what? You gonna be alright. The only thing you can see right now, because it's right now, is everything that you're going through is bad, but I'mma tell you something real important. Your future is brighter.*" Your future is brighter than this moment. Like I always tell you—tomorrow's gonna be better than yesterday, but you just gotta hold on. Stay dedicated. Keep going at what you know is inside of you. Keep going after that. I'm telling you—do not give up on yourself. Your future is brighter than what you see right now. And it's just like that!

4.24.2018

It's Not About Who Likes It

What's important is, it's not about who like it, it's about if *you* like it. Whatever you doing in life, whether it's fashion, whether it's food, whether it's going on a trip—whatever—it's about if *you* like it. We gotta stop letting people think for us. We'll go off of things like, *"oh—they like that? That's what they doing? So that's what I like"* No. You can't think for me, I'mma think for me. That's what the reality of life is. It's not about who like it, it's about if you like it. What do you like? What do you wanna do? Who do you wanna be? Be that. Be that! But stop letting other people think for you. *"Oh no—this restaurant over here, it's poppin'."* Who said it was poppin'? Did you taste the food yet? So you let all these people, because it's a big crowd going there, make the decision for you and you never even tasted the food. How you know you like the food? It's not about who like it, it's about if you like it. You gotta like the things that you put into your body. The things, the places you go, the clothes. You gotta like them. Stop letting people dictate the pace for you. Stop letting people be the director of your life. You're the director. You're the screenwriter. And you're the actor and the star of the movie of your life and it's just like that!

4.24.2018

Know Your Rooms

What rooms you wanna be in? And you gotta do your research before you get in the rooms, so when you get in the room you grab the attention of all the people that's occupying the room so you can stay in the room. But you know we always say, *"I wanna go here, I wanna go here."* What rooms do you really wanna get into? Or you just wanna get into a room to get you the bag to get you some paper? No. Every room is not for you. Listen—every meeting is not for you. Find out what rooms and meetings are for you to where as though you can bring value to those rooms and meetings and they say, you know what—we gotta keep you here because you add value to what we got going on. But you gotta understand the room that you wanna be in. It's a bunch of rooms in this world that you wanna be in. But you gotta figure out, every room ain't for you. Every room is not gonna be receptive to what you got going on. Find the rooms that's receptive to what you got going on whereas though you can add something to these rooms, make these rooms stronger, and make the people in the room wanna keep you. Do your research—that's what Google is for. Do your research. I done been to meetings with people and I be like, "How's the dog doing?" He like, *"Oh, how'd you know..."* Yeah—I know my stuff. "I see you were sick last week. How's everything? You better now?" Know the rooms you're walking into before you walk into the rooms that you say you wanna be in. And it's just like that!

4.25.2018

Grind Activates Shine

That grind activates the shine! You might look and say, *"WOWW, LOOK. Shine Avenue—I'm going there."* Go gotta go through Grind Boulevard in order to get to Shine Boulevard! And let me tell you something! You gotta embrace that. You gotta embrace that struggle. You gotta embrace that grind and you gotta turn it up. 'Cause I'mma tell you something. When the grind come and you know you really on your grind is when that change activate that pain and when that pain is activated, that's when the shine is getting closer.

I don't care who you is, everybody we look at, *"oh they winning. I wanna be like them"* Let me tell you something before Oprah got where she got to, LIFE KICKED HER ASS!! Life was kicking Oprah's ass! But you know what? She stayed ten toes down in her position and she kept grinding! She kept grinding and now she shining. I don't care who you are. I don't care what you doing out there. Remember this: if you talk about shine, you better be talking about grind! And it's just like THAT!

4.26.2018

Watch Energy, Not Words

See the reality is, you gotta respect energy, not words. You gotta watch energy, not words. Sometimes somebody will tell you something and be like, "Ahhhh," you don't even be feeling it. You know why? Because their words and their energy don't align. Their energy might be bad, but the words might *sound* good, but it don't align. You feel it. You be like, "hol', hol' up—I can't be receptive to that. Yeah it's cool what you saying. Yeah I understand what you saying, yeah. That's alright, yeah…" And that's how you be. Because you can't embrace that. You can't internalize what they're saying because it don't align with the energy that they're producing when they're saying what they're saying. Think about that. Watch energy, not words. Respect energy, not words. The words are nothing. They're just a small thing. The words are just like the plate, but it's not the food. So you gotta remember this: every time that you hear somebody say something to you, check the alignment and say hol'—do it match the energy? Do it match the energy that's supposed to be matching these words? If it don't—keep moving. And it's just... like... that!!

4.26.2018

Network to Create a Movement

You can't teach what you don't know and you can't lead where you don't go. We're trying to figure out, damn, how are gonna stop mass-incarceration, how we gonna do this, I wanna do that... You gotta network. Like Les Brown says: your network equals your net worth. What you gotta do is, if you're trying to create a movement, number one, you gotta know how to navigate the machine—the biggest machine we have on Earth. Some people say, *"Oh I ain't have no money, I..."* I came out of prison—I ain't have no money, but I had the machine. The machine is everything. This is the machine (holds up iPhone). Whatever you trying to do, whatever message you trying to get across, all you need is this.

But you gotta understand your network equals your net worth and you gotta network with people. And all those strangers out there, you gotta know how to connect with people in a nanosecond. Because our attention is being grabbed because so much stuff is coming to us every day. So you gotta learn how to connect with the people and create a movement. And how you create a movement is you gotta know your strengths. You gotta respect your strengths and you gotta respect your weaknesses. And you gotta connect with the people that's in the field that you say you're trying to be in. Everybody here, I need you to connect with somebody here and travel through life with them. Don't leave here and don't connect with nobody. Don't come here and just say you went there and take the pictures. No that's cool, you can take pictures. What we gotta stop doing is we gotta stop fronting. See, that Instagram bio and all these social media is killing us because we create a lie for ourselves and we start believing the lie. And we gotta understand something that's real important: The lie is the new religion and attention is the new currency. So you got all these people, they can give you these cards, *"Oh here's my card, I'm such and such."* You ain't do nothing. What did you do? What impact have you made? You got feet on the ground? Or do you just got this illusion that you built up for yourself? We don't wanna get caught up in building illusions. We need to build businesses. And we need to build movements.

In order to build a movement you gotta connect with the people that can strengthen the movement. If you ain't been to prison and you're trying to do something with reentry—get somebody that's been to prison that could be the mouthpiece because they've got that lived experience, you don't. So there's a disconnect there. If you're trying to get into music, get with someone that's been in the music business that will connect you to the people you say you're trying to connect with.

4.27.2018

I Was 4 Different People

See I used to be four different people. I wanted to get money like him. I wanted to get the women like him. I wanted to be fly like him. And I wanted to be tough like him.

I'm talking about my back used to be hurting because I was carrying around all these multiple identities. 'Cause I was just all over the place. It used to be crazy because I had to switch at different moments, ya know? I'd go from trying to get the women and all of a sudden I'm being tough and I used to be jumping all over the place being these different people. Four people in one? That's a crazy lifestyle, but that's the lifestyle I was living. But when I tapped in and started being me, that's when I became free.

I was in a prison cell, but I became free. That was the freest I had ever been sitting in a cell. Because it was like, alright here I am in a cell, but I finally connected with who I truly was. 'Cause all the other time I was living a lie. I was frauding—I was pump-faking as everybody would say. And when I became me, that's when my life changed. That's when the world opened up to me and everything just started flowing through. And I became me.

4.27.2018

When You Know Who a Person is, You Don't Have to Worry

When you know who a person is, you don't have to worry about it. We spend so much time worrying about people. If you know these people over here love you, you don't have to worry about it. If you know these people over here do not like you, do not mess with you—you don't have to worry about it. We gotta take people for who they are once we say, okay, "I know y'all on my team, I know y'all not." That's it. Don't be focused on, "*oh you ain't on my team—why you hating, why you...*" No, don't worry about them. You don't have to worry about them no more. Now you know, okay cool. I ain't gotta deal with you, I ain't gotta put no more energy over here. I can put my energy onto y'all because I know y'all my supporters, y'all with me. Thank you. I appreciate y'all people. I don't appreciate who I don't got, but I appreciate who I do got. And I'm not gonna give time or energy to the people that I don't got. Over here, it's gonna go to y'all and it's gonna go to me materializing my dreams and going forward to what I need to be. That's what it's about. If you know who a person is, you don't have to worry about them. And it's just… like… THAT!

4.29.2018

Peeking and Ain't Speaking

Every time you looking at your Instagram story and you see all these people's names on your Insta-story and you say to yourself, why they keep peeking and they ain't speaking? Calm down don't worry about them speaking. They don't need to speak to you, 'cause you know what? They're a viewer of the movie of your life. You're the star of the show—they're watching a movie. They're watching your movie. You got them so tuned into your movie they just be like, "Unh, dag!" Whether they're hating or they not, don't even worry about that. They're a viewer to your network. They're watching your show so don't worry about them peeking and they ain't speaking. They just doing a drive-by. 'Cause you keep saying to yourself, damn I keep seeing their name… And then you keep seeing the views so you saying to yourself why. Don't worry about who ain't speaking, as long as they peeking. That means you got something going on, baby. You're a winner out here, you're doing something. 'Cause I'm not going nowhere and I'm not watching nothing that ain't doing nothing. I'm not even gonna be tuned into it if I don't like it. See they really like you, but they don't know how to say hi 'cause they afraid 'cause you're the star of the show. And the movie is about you. And it's just like THAT!

5.1.2018

Don't Fear Numbers on the Internet

"They get all these likes, they get all these views. Oh they're better than me." No they not! They're not better than you. Stop putting people on these pedestals. Just because somebody got a large following—I know people that don't even got social media that's doing way better than people with these hundreds of thousands of followers. Because a lot of people is faking, they ain't making. They faking it. They aint making it. You see a picture of somebody leaning on a car or somebody in a different city. That don't mean that they there to make nothing happen. That mean they might be there for vacation, but they might try to convince you that they making something happen and that don't mean nothing. Stop being afraid of people on

the internet and putting everybody on a pedestal higher than you. And saying that they value is worth more than yours when that's not the reality of this. Don't get numbers mixed up. It ain't about how many followers you got, it's about who following you. Are the move-makers and the shakers that can change life following you? If you're in an arena to make something happen whether music, fashion or whatever? C'mon! Stop being afraid of people on the internet. You see a girl that you like—go right at her! You see somebody that's handsome—go right at him! But don't think people on the internet because they have large numbers that they're doing better than you, because there's a lot of people that are not on the internet that're doing better than the people with the large numbers, and it's just like THAT!

5.2.2018

Use Your Words Carefully

Use your words carefully. Your mouth-piece is the key to every closed door on the planet Earth. Think about this. Good conversation, good communication, leads to good situations. Bad conversation, bad communication, leads to bad situations. We be in there talking about this, just talking—you don't know who you're offending. You don't know who you're talking to—to somebody they might be connected to, to somebody that might can help you. But you know what? That's why you gotta be mindful and you gotta utilize your mouth-piece the proper way. Think about it. Connect your mind to your mouth when you're utilizing your mouth, let your mind dictate and control your mouth and the game will change. Don't just be running your mouth, *"blah, blah, blah, blah, blah."* 'Cause you gotta pay attention to what I said, it's very important: good communication, good conversation, leads to good situations. Listen—this, our mouth-piece, is the only thing that we have. You wonder why this person over there, doing well, and this person is over there doing big things. Because they know how to utilize their mouth and connect it to their mind and speak mindfully. Your mouth-piece is the key to every closed door on the planet Earth!

5.2.2018

Delete Them Out Your Phone

No—the way my life is set up, I prioritize. So it's things that I gotta handle for me and what's going on with my situation so I can't do that for you right now. No, I'm just saying no right now. Nahmean?

All the people in your life that you say 'no' to and they only call you and every time they call you they calling you with an ask—they never call you to check on you, your family or to see what's going on? Delete them out your phone right now. And then they have the nerve that when you say no, they don't call you. You don't hear from them. They got an attitude. Delete them out your phone. They don't deserve to be in your phone because they're not for you. Have people on your phone that's for you. Not people that it's only about them. It's always about them. *"Oh yeah, could you do this for me?"* No, I ain't doing it. No. No. And it ain't no reason why, it's just no. Because you always calling about you. It's never about me, it's always about you. And it's never mutually beneficial, it's always about you. So no, you're not in my phone and when you call my phone, so they can have this in their mind, when you call my phone I don't know the number no more 'cause you out my phone. You dig what I'm saying? And it's just like *that!*

5.4.2018

Copy & Paste ≠ Success

No, no, no! That's not the way it go. You can't copy and paste your way to success. You're thinking because, *"Oh no—what they got going on, oh they winning! You know what I'mma do? I'mma mimic everything they got going on. I'mma take their template and just put my information in it and it's gonna work for me."* That's not how life works! Everybody's journey is different. The route that you may take to California, I may take a different one. Everybody's destination is different. Everybody's journey is different. You can't copy and paste your way to success. *"Oh—they got real estate. I'm gonna do exactly what they're doing and I'mma win."* You just might now win. You might take a lot of losses. The contractors might just don't come through for you the way they come through for them. You can't copy and paste your way to success! You gotta put your hustle in! You gotta grind! That's what you gotta do. And you gotta find ingenious ways to make something happen. All these ideas we do? Everybody doing the same thing, but you got different routes. So you can't copy and paste your way to success! And it's just like that!!

5.4.2018

The Bottom Dictates Culture

See it's about the bottom respecting you. See, the bottom, once they respect you—once the people at the bottom respect you from where you come from, they are gonna push you up so you can get the attention of the people at the top. Because the top only respects what the bottom respects. The bottom dictates everything. You might think, "*Oh only the people at the top...*" No, no, no—in order for them to get your attention is because the people at the bottom are screaming up to them, "*Look! Look! This is what's poppin'! This is what's going on.*" You can't finesse your way to the top, it's not gonna go that way. The people at the bottom run this thing. They run everything. So you'll be sitting there saying to yourself,

"Oh I'mma take this…"—Ain't no shortcuts to the top, baby. Ain't no shortcuts. The people at the top only respect the people at the bottom. They are the ones that dictate the pace. They're the ones that dictate culture. The people at the bottom. And once they respect you, it's a wrap. That's when you got the game together—when the people at the bottom respect you.

5.6.2018

Divorce the Lie

Oh you in love, huh? You in love. The marriage coming up, huh? You done fell in love with that lie. The lie that you created for yourself. The lie that your relationship is good when it's not. The lie that you really winning when you not. The lie that you're rich and all 'cause you got this material when you not. The lie that you created for social media. The lie that you created to your family. The lie that you created at work. You just created this big ole lie and you fell in love with the lie and now y'all married, huh? You better get a divorce! You better get a divorce! You better get a divorce because if you keep being in love, you keep being married and dedicated to this lie—nothing right is gonna come your way! Because you're not gonna be focused. This lie is gonna have your mind all clouded with all this other stuff. Because you're believing that you're somebody that you're not. You believing that your situation is something that it's not. You believing that you're happy when you're not. C'mon! You believing in that lie, huh? You love that lie, huh? You married to that lie, huh? Yeah, I sound like Juvenile now, huh?! Yeah—you better divorce that lie and stop playing. You better divorce it. Get a divorce. And it's just like that!

5.7.2018

When the Plate Get Bigger the Hate Get Bigger

This what you said you wanted! You said you wanted to go to the next levels of life! The plate got bigger so the hate got bigger! Hol'! It ain't you! You ain't changing, they changing. As you elevating they contemplating ways to start something with you so they can be out of place with you because they're uncomfortable with your success. You know why? Because they probably thought they supposed to have your success. But no. You put the work in for your success, so now that your plate getting bigger, the hate getting bigger. All these arguments. All these disagreements. All these plots and plans to just be out of position with you due to the fact that you're winning. But you gotta understand when the plate get bigger, the hate get bigger. Listen—and when you elevating they contemplating ways to make things shake up. They just not comfortable with your success. They say they love you, but you know what? Actions speak louder than words. And they words ain't matching their actions. 'Cause you know what? When you start elevating they start contemplating ways to break it up with you. What's important more than anything: When your plate get bigger the hate get bigger so you better prepare yourself if you want your plate to get bigger. You gotta deal with this and it's just like that!

5.7.2018

You Can Accept Praise but Can You Accept Being Checked?

Actions speak louder than words. When you making it happen, you making it happen. At the end of the day, if you're an entrepreneur, you're supposed to be decorating the interiors of your bank account, not yourself. Think about that. Think about the Gucci and all the Louis you got. And say to yourself, I got all these bags, I got all these shoes, I got all these belts, but I ain't got that type of money in my business account. If I write a check it might bounce like a basketball in the playoffs. See everybody always—we have all these meetings, we have all these celebrations to give people this award and that award, but are we really putting the work in that's necessary to make it happen out here in this world? That's the question. Because it's cool to give props—it's cool for somebody to say you doing your thing, you got it going on, I like the way you look, I like this, that, and the third, but could you deal with when somebody checks you?

5.8.2018

Your Real Life Vs. Their Fake Life

C'mon man. C'mon, what you talking 'bout? You living a real life. Think about this. You really go to work everyday. You really take care of your kids everyday. You really go to school everyday. You really handle your business everyday. And you comparing your *real* life to somebody's fake life on Instagram? Is you kidding me?! You comparing your life to filters. Think about that. You comparing your life to minutes. Your whole life and the real things that you got going on, you're comparing them to a minute? Or, I'm talking about a second, or half of a second clip? Is you kidding me? Think about that. C'mon—you really need to check yourself. If you're comparing your *whole* life—you really got real things that you doing, you really going through real situations, you're really motivated by this and by that—and you're comparing that to one minute? Somebody's fake life that they done put together and you comparing that. To a filter? Stop comparing your real life to somebody's fake life on Instagram. And it's just like that!

5.8.2018

Your Dreams Belong to You

No, No, NO! You better not stop, you hear me? You better not stop going after what belongs to you. That's yours! That dream, them dreams that you have? They belong to you, they're your property. You have the deed to them dreams. Go get your property. Go claim yours. Don't let it just sit there. Don't let somebody else use it as a band-ominium. Use your dream and just be squatting in there. That's your dream, you hear me? That's your deed. Go get your property! Stop playing games. You better never stop. You better never give up on what belongs to you! You got ownership of that. That's yours! It's in your name, but it's waiting for your arrival. It's sitting there with a tag right here with your name on it. Like, you know how you go to the airport and they be standing there with the names? The driver waiting there? It's waiting for you. Your dream is like this, "Come on, Kev. Come on, Michael. Come on, Billy. Come on, Michelle. Come on, Kareem. Come on, Debbie. Come on, Jill. Come on, _________." That's how it's waiting for you! You better never stop, you hear me? 'Cause I ain't gon' never stop. And it's just like that!!

5.14.2018

The Receipt Holders

You gotta be wary of those people, every time they give to you, they always looking for a receipt. They wanna keep this receipt for those days so later on when you do whatever you got going on, they can say, *"Oh I've done this for you. I've done that for you. I've done this, I've done that, I've done that, I've done this."* Be wary of them. Yeah—you know who I'm talking about. They just wanna keep record of what they've done for you 'cause they ain't do it genuinely. It wasn't genuine. It was based off of what they gon' get later on from you. It was based off when they can cash this in. How you gon' cash in something that you gave to somebody? Think about that. So those people that hold those receipts that you know we got in our life—get away from them. They keep holding receipts. They got a big bag of receipts on everybody. They always got something to say, *"Oh I did this for them, I did that for them..."* Get away from them receipt holders.

And it's just like that!

5.14.2018

Your Grind is Everything

One thing that you gotta understand is that your grind is the interior decorator of your bank account. Your grind is the stylist of your bank account. Don't get caught up in popularity on social media. 'Cause you'll see somebody with 200,000 followers and you'll say, *"Oh they're making it happen! I need this many followers to win."* That's not true 'cause a lot of people with 200,000 followers, they ain't got a quarter in their bank account for every follower. So if you got 200,000 followers, you 'sposed to have $50,000 in your bank account. Hol' up—let me downplay that. Let me just say you have ten cent for every follower you got, that's $20,000. A lot of people don't have that. So don't get caught up and say if I ain't got this many followers, I can't win. There's people out here with 1,500 followers or 1,000 followers, that's really monetizing and they're converting their followers into customers. Everybody's not doing that. Let me tell you something. A lot of people with all these numbers, they got people that be stopping, but they ain't shopping. They got people that be peeking, but they ain't speaking. So don't get caught up in that and think you need all these followers to make it happen. What you need is that grind. The grind is everything. And it's just like that!

5.14.2018

Everything You Need is Here

C'mon stop playing games. You keep talking about I'm trying to get into the building and all this, "I need the people to bring me in. I want to get a deal with them. I want to get a deal with them." Everything you need is right here (holds up iPhone). All the service you need if you do music, right here this is your distributor. Right here, if you sell merch. Right here, Shopify, you can do whatever. You sell clothes, you got a clothing line, right here. This is where you connect with all the manufacturers, the people you need—it's right here in this phone. You keep talking about I need to get with this person, no you need to get with your phone. Every resource that you want, everybody that you trying to connect with is right here in your phone. All the money you need is right here in your phone. Chief Keef was on two months house arrest when he shot a video and it went viral. He was on house arrest. You ain't on house arrest and if you is on house arrest, you can make it happen, but more than likely you ain't on house arrest. Think about it. Everything that I ever established, only thing I had was this phone. Crib, I got everything now. I don't have to worry about no paper or none of that, because of this. Them checks are being cut from universities, everybody that's booking me—all because of this. Everything was established on this. You gotta start taking advantage of this and stop playing games. Listen, this is the trap so start trapping and it's just like that!

5.18.2018

Challenge Yourself

See you gotta challenge yourself—you hear me?. You gotta challenge yourself. I don't care about who you think you are today, you gotta continually challenge yourself on who you was yesterday. Every day, when I wake up, I'm not Wallo267. I gotta earn that name. I gotta earn Wallo267 every day 'cause I gotta prove to myself that I'm not the old Wallo. Because when decisions come, when some of the decisions come, I gotta make sure that old way of thinking is not gonna pop up and try to make me be Wallo instead of Wallo267. That's where the challenge comes. You gotta challenge yourself every day in order to earn who you say you are today. But you know what? You know what makes these decisions even stronger? Because I support Wallo267 with the people, places, and things that I'm around. Now if I was around the people, places, and things of Wallo, it'd have been a different time, but I support that. You gotta challenge yourself. And it's just like that!

5.20.2018

Affiliation Will Will Your Situation

Let me tell you something that's very important: affiliation will kill your situation. You'll be sitting here thinking, damn I'm almost there, I'm almost at the finish line. And then you get there and you don't get that callback or somebody don't reach out no more. You know why? It's about who you affiliated with. It ain't about you got great talent—you know you got the talent. *"Damn I wanna take it to the next level. Why I ain't take it to the next..."* Who you got around you? Who you affiliated with? The same thing—you'll be trying to get into certain rooms and no ain't nobody dealing with that nut stuff. At the end of the day, if you saying you trying to go left, but they going right, it's just not gon' happen. Who do you deal with? The people that you deal with will keep closed doors closed. And they won't open them because they're like, "*nahh—something ain't right with this guy because if he deal with them and they knuckleheads or she deal with them and they knuckleheads… no, no—***she** *gotta be a knucklehead,* **he** *gotta be a knucklehead.*" Affiliation will kill your situation. You saying to yourself, why this ain't happen? Who you got around you? Affiliation will kill your situation. And it's just like that!

5.22.2018

Brains & Bread

See the reality is, it's two things that gotta come together like peanut butter and jelly, if you got an idea you got the brains, but you also need the bread in order to bring your idea alive. Brains… bread. Bread… brains. Then you got people that got the bread, but they don't have the brains to take their bread to another level. Alright you got money, but sometimes you gotta collaborate with an individual that got the brains that can make your money breakdance. That can make your money do backflips. That can make your money make money when you sleeping. That can make your money make money, make money, make money, and make money when you sleeping. But brains and bread go together like peanut butter and jelly. That's the problem. We always trying to make it happen, *"Oh yeah I got all these ideas,"*—oh sooo what?! You got all these ideas, but you need to collaborate with other people so you can enhance your ideas and get it off from being an idea—get it off that paper, get it off that blueprint into reality. That's what it is. But it gotta be brains… bread. 'Cause brains and bread gotta connect so if you got the brains, find the bread. If you got the bread, find the brains 'cause y'all two can't exist without each other. And it's just like that!

5.23.2018

Fix Your F#%King Clock!

You keep playing games! You keep playing! *"Oh, oh! My clock broke—I can't go no more. I don't know what time it is..."* You know what time it is!! You broke your clock!! You got complacent and said, *"Oh I made it far enough, I can't go no farther. I'm in my comfort zone."* Fix your fucking clock!!! Keep moving!! Why you gon' stop?! You got a whole life to go at! Oh—you driving? You know you gotta go a hundred miles! You stop at 25, or you stop at 35, or you stop at 45 miles, park up in a rest stop! You got a full tank of gas and you know you gotta reach the destination, but you got scared! 'Cause you got comfortable! You got in that comfort zone. You got complacent. GET UP!! Keep moving!! Start that car back up!! And fix your fucking clock! And it's just like that!!

5.24.2018

Get Out of Your World

The reality is, you gotta get out of your world in order to see the world. A lot of times we think everything that goes on in our little small world exists in the main world. Naw You keep doing that, you gon' be running late. Your world is cool. Your world is just one little minute, I'm talking about minute, I'm talking the size of an ant, mindset in the approach to life. The way that you see it in your world, your neighborhood, your family with your—naw that don't exist in the big world. And you wonder why you running late and you not relatable to everybody else in the world. Because you can't see the world 'cause you gotta get out of your world in order to see the world. But you never gon' get out of your world because you so think this is the approach. You're so comfortable. You're so comfortable that you're not relatable to the whole world and what goes on around the world. 'Cause you think only the culture that you have in your community or your section or wherever you at exists. Naw. That's why you running late. You always gon' be running late and you never gon' be able to relate to the world, everybody else in different cultures and different places. Get out of your world in order to see the world, or you always gon' be running late. And it's just like that!

5.27.2018

Overthinking Killed Your Plan

What is you doing? You keep talking about, "I'm thinking this, I'm putting this plan together, thinking..." You thinking so much. Thinking can harm you sometimes. We think, "Aw man, I'm thinking, I'm making it happen, that's gon' make..." That don't mean nothing. Sometimes you can think so long, that you'll come up with a way to think your way out of making it happen. Out of moving out on what you were thinking about 'cause you just been thinking and strategizing for so long because you got so smart that you're dumb. "I got it together, I'm getting this plan together." Okay, the plan, okay. You done finessed your way out of the plan because you thought so much. You thought so much that you done became paralyzed by thinking and the only thing you fell in love with is thinking and that's your whole way of moving out. "Yeah I'm thinking, yeah I'm doing this." You're over-strategizing. Stop over-strategizing and move out. Stop finessing yourself out of action. So much thought, but it's no action. You got all this thought, you thinking all this stuff. All so smart, reading all this stuff, but you ain't doing shit. That's the reality of it. When you gon' start moving out and really doing something? And stop overthinking? And it's just like that!

5.29.2018

Fake Has Us All Traumatized & Confused

Fake got you traumatized now. You know why? 'Cause social media killed reality and none of us showed up to the funeral because fake jumped on the stream. Fake was Goldie. Fake was this extraordinary mack. I'm taking 'bout fake was just this mack that came through, put his wordplay down on us, had us all in a trance, and next thing we know, we on the track. We hoes on the street corner now for fake. You know why? 'Cause fake is just so powerful. Fake is everything. Fake is the new god. Yeah, think about that. Yeah—you worship him every day. Every move you make, every time you go to post, you alter this. Every time you go to put this on and you put this on and it's just not who you really are. It's just add this or add that or take this or take that, but it's fake. But you convinced that it's real. And anybody that come to you about the fakeness? They're fake, they're not real and they're a hater. Because real don't exist in this world. Real is dead. I seen real's funeral come up, but I ain't even go. I seen the obituary, but real—real is corny, real is slain, real is fake, fake is fake, fake is real… I don't even know…

5.29.2018

Follow After You

I don't care who you follow. I don't care who you listen to, but what's important—ain't nobody A, B, C is gon' get you D. Only your A, B, C is gon' get you D. You gotta understand that. Stop worrying about what everybody else is doing. Nobody's life is gonna dictate yours. Nobody's life is gonna impact yours. Only your life and the way you move out is gonna impact yours. Stop playing games. Nobody's A, B, C is gonna get you D. Only your A, B, C is gonna get you D. No matter what you going through, when you going through it, just keep going through it. But I'mma tell you one thing: you gotta follow after you. Long as you follow after you, everything is gonna be perfect. Everything is gonna go your way. Everything, everything, everything. Nobody's A, B, C is gonna get you D—only yours. And it's just like that!

9.5.2018

The Corner

Now you're live here at 13th and Allegheny. This is the street corner where I started my whole stunts and I started getting into the street game. Come on with me. Let me show you something that's very important. See this right here? Most of my OGs, most of my homies, we stood right here on this corner—the majority of them are dead. OG Rundy, Boogie Down, my big brother, the list goes on... Kendell, Man-Man, everybody dead or they in the penitentiary doing a bunch of time. We used to be posted up—this used to be a Chinese store, but we used to be posted up here. You know how many times people came through and shot the block up? Because somebody was standing here with us that'd done something? Then they slide up on the block and we don't know? The corner is dangerous. It's real dangerous so you gotta move and groove—you gotta know that. Because ain't nobody gonna tell you they just done some slick shit. Ain't nobody gon' tell you they just robbed somebody, they just shot somebody. They'll come right here and post up with you—you sitting on the crate and somebody come through and spray the block. You gotta be on point. I'm talking 'bout corners all across America. You gotta be on point, man. I'm just giving you the game as it was given to me. I'm Wallo267, I'm talking about the corner and it's just like that!

9.7.2018

Don't Do Popular, Do You

What you doing? What you doing? Don't do what's popular—do what's you. What is the matter with you? Why you think that things are just not working for you, they just not coming through for you? You know why? 'Cause you not doing you. Don't do what's popular, do what's you. You keep, *"aww they did this over here so I'm gonna do...* " Whatever you doing, whether in fashion, whether in music, whether in the restaurant business, whether in hair—don't do what's popular, do what's you! You biting off of them. What they're doing is working for them because that's them. That's their thing, it's not your thing! C'mon man. *"Oh he wrapped up with his videos a certain way, if his video that way"*—that's his thing, that's what he do! C'mon man, you trying to mimic. *"Oh they do their clothes like this"*—that's what they do, that's their thing. Don't do what's popular, do what's you. Everything you do is based off of what you think is gonna pop. No—your truth is gonna pop! That's what pop! Your truth! Being somebody else don't pop! Don't do what's popular, do what's you. And it's just like that!

9.8.2018

When You're On or When You're Gone

People only love you when you're on or when you're gone. So once they see that you got to that place of success or that finance is there, they like, *"Oh they made it, they poppin'. Let me jump on that and support that."* Because it's fashionable to support a person when they on, but when they going through the struggle, it's not fashionable to support them. People only love you when you're on or when you're gone. Go to a funeral, you see all these people. You be like damnn—whatshisname knew this many people? Did he have something going on? Was all these people supporting what he had going on? 'Cause if they were supporting what he had going on he might still be living. People only love you when you're gone or when you're on. So in reality, they don't really love you—it's just fashionable to do. It's fashionable to support a person that really don't need the support no more because they done made it. They done put that work in and they done made it to the next level. But a person that's on the grind, they don't support them. And, you know you gotta go to a funeral. You gotta post them up—that's the way, that's like the dress code, the new thing, it's fashionable. People only love you when you're on or when you're gone and it's just like that!

9.9.2018

The Blame Game

Stop worrying about about what people ain't doing for you and start worrying about what you ain't doing for you. You'll sit back and base your life, whether you win or whether you lose in life, off the moves somebody might've made for you or the moves somebody didn't make for you. And you'll blame them because you're losing in life. But you never take accountability that you ain't do everything that you needed to do to take it to the next levels of life. That you ain't put that overtime in that you needed to put into yourself so you can make things happen in life. No, you'll say, *"so-and-so ain't do this for me, so-and-so aint' do this, so-and-so."* So you'll put your life in somebody else's hands?! Stop worrying about what somebody ain't do for you and start blaming yourself for the things you ain't do for yourself to take life to the next level. You won't do that. It's everybody's fault. *"Oh I'm losing in life. Things ain't going right for me. Oh this, oh that. He done this, she done this. They ain't do this."* Stop bullshittin'. Stop playing games. And blame yourself for not making it happen the way you need to make it happen for yourself in order to take it to the next levels. And it's just like *that!*

9.14.2018

Burnt Out

(Standing in front of a completely burned down building)

Sometimes you're just gonna get burnt out. You're gonna get burnt out by life. You're gonna get burnt out by relationships. You're gonna get burnt out by just a lot of things: family, friends, but it's cool to get burnt out. It's cool—you know why? Because now after you get burnt out you can rebuild. You can start over. Nothing is wrong with starting over. Nothing is wrong with being burnt out. You ever say to yourself, *"Oh they burning me out. I'm burnt out from this, I'm burnt out from that."* It's cool to be burnt out from that. It's cool to be burnt out—that's okay. Burnt out means a brand new start. Burnt out mean a brand new beginning. Because everything that was there is just done. Now you got, look at this—you can rebuild this. Get all the rubbish, get all the stuff outta here and start to rebuild. Start to build the new you. Start to rebuild the new journey. Start to rebuild the new relationships. It's cool to be burnt out. And it's just like that!

9.18.2018

Experience Is Your Best Friend

People come and go, but experiences live forever. Don't worry about who came in your life and who's not there no more. Connect with the experiences you had when that person was in your life. People come in our lives. They might stay momentarily, they might stay longer, but it's about the experience we have with the people that come in our lives. That's the biggest gain—that's your best friend. The experience. The experience you connect with when you're with that person. When that person is traveling through life with you. That's the most important thing. Experience. *"Oh they not here. Ohhh."* Don't worry about that. Don't worry about that a person moved on.

Worry about the game that you got when that person was in your life. That's what you worry about. Worry about that. That's the most important thing than anything. Game. Guidance, attention, motivation, education. That's the experience. The things that this person that was in your life exposed you to. That's the things that you learned when this person was in your life. That's more important than anything. Experience is your best friend. Understand that. And it's just like that.

9.19.2018

It's Never Too Late

The reality is, it's never too late to be who you would have been. Let me say this again: it's never too late to be who you would have been. You're breathing so who are you, or anybody else to put an expiration date on your dream. Huh? How you gon' give up on who you always said you wanted to be? You said, *"I ain't got time. Oh, I got older. Oh, I got kids. Oh, I got this. Oh, I got that. Oh, I been to jail. Oh, I was on drugs. Oh, I was this."* So what?! Don't you ever put an expiration date on your dreams and the things that you always imagined that you wanted to be. Or the things that you said you wanna do. Stop doing that. Nothing. Nothing can stop you, but you. You gotta remember this. You still breathing. You got a chance to win. You got a chance to do anything you wanna do. Hol'! Did your time run out? Hol'—you're not in the grave.

Hol'—why you complaining? C'mon stop playing games. And stop putting an expiration date on your dreams. And stop saying that you can't do this. And stop convincing yourself and letting others convince you that you can't make everything that you said you wanted to be, come true. And it's just like that!

9.23.2018

From the Inside Out

You're not gonna be able to do what you wanna do, unless you already done what you needed to do. And what you needed to do, was cleanse your soul. Clean your insides out. We'll say, I'm on this, I'm trying to start this business, I'm reading this, I'm going to work, I'm gonna do this, that, and the third. Naw! The inside starts before anything. If your insides are right, your outsides are gon' be right. You still got the judgment. You still got the anger from yesterday. You still got the envy in you. You still all worried about hurt that's gone. You still angry about people that don't even exist in your life no more. You got all this stuff going on. You don't have no space to be receptive to the new things that you say you want in life. You can't go nowhere. You can't move. 'Cause even when you go somewhere, you're still stuck in the place of yesterday. You're still stuck in that angry moment. You're still stuck in that judgmental mindset. You're stuck in all the stuff that don't got nothing to do with you going to the next levels of life or you growing. That's why you can't grow, and that's why you ain't gon' be able to go. Take care of your insides and once your insides are right, your outside's gonna be right. And it's just like that!

9.27.2018

Get Away From Yes People

You gotta get away from the yes people. You keep holding on to the yes people. The people that the only thing they do is support any idea you got, even if the idea is goofy. You gotta surround yourself with people that don't need you. People that don't need you to pay their bills, they don't need to be around you for recognition, they don't need you for nothing. Because they're gonna force you to go to the next levels of life and they're not gonna cosign the goofy ideas and the goofy moves that you're gonna make. The only people that are gonna cosign that are the people that need you. They need to be around you. Listen—you better get away from them. 'Cause you know what? You gonna crash and burn, baby! You gon' crash and burn. You gon' be taken out of the air, you gon' burn. BOOM! Explosive! 'Cause you know what, you gotta get away from them yes-men. And women, you better get away from them yes-women. And start getting around people that don't need you. And it's just like that!

9.28.2018

Listen While You're Winning

You gotta learn how to listen while you winning. You sitting there and you saying to yourself, "*Oh I'm winning. I got the cars. I got the jewels. I got the women. I got the money. I'm winning! I'm winning, I'm winning, I'm winning!*" Yeah you winning, but you better listen while you winning. See that's the problem—we only wanna listen when we lose. So as soon as the winning stop, "*Oh we're not in the championship this year. We're not going to the playoffs.*" Now you wanna sit there and listen to the coach. Now you wanna sit there and listen to your trainer. You gotta listen while you winning. I told you this before, but I know you aint peep game. You ain't peep the game. You gotta listen while you winning in order to keep winning. That's how the great champions, stay champions. The great champions, stay champions because they listen to their teammates. They listen to the players that's not getting the money that they're getting—that's pushing them, that's encouraging them, that's helping them get to the next levels of life. You gotta listen while you winning to keep winning. That's how the champions stay champions. ***And it's just like that!***

10.3.2018

Don't Beef with Information

Because they got a problem with you, that don't mean you can't take no information from them. It was this one cat when I was in the joint, me and him, we had a bunch of disagreements—we wasn't feeling each other. We was cool, but we wasn't dealing with each other on no level. But one time, I'm sitting inside my cell and he was outside my cell hollering at somebody and he gave this bul the best game of life. The information was everything. Just because you're beefing with somebody or you don't like somebody, that don't mean you gotta be beefing with the information, 'cause you'll miss out on some top flight game. You'll be missing out because emotions cloud reactions and sometimes you might see a woman doing her thing, sis, and you'll be like, *"oh I don't like her"*—that don't mean the information that she's giving out, or the game that she's giving out or how she's approaching her business or whatever can't help you. Don't get so emotionally inclined to shut down on everything—naw! Indirectly they could be giving you game even if you don't like each other. So don't beef with the information. You got beef with the person, beef with *them*, but just be open minded because it's game everywhere and anybody can give you game. And it's just like that!

10.3.2018

Kill That Entitlement

That entitlement is why you ain't where you wanna be at! You think everybody owe you something! *"Oh they supposed to done this. Why they ain't do this? They should've done this for me. They should've done this..."*. Why you ain't do it for yourself? Why you ain't make it happen for yourself? 'Cause you think that everything that you say you want, somebody supposed to deliver it to you. And if you don't get it delivered, where they knock on your door—"Excuse me" (Knock, knock, knock, knock) and you come to the door with your robe on—you don't want it! You don't want it! You gotta put that work in. Put that work in. Don't nobody owe you nothing! I gotta keep telling people this. Everybody think—I don't *care* if they're from your neighborhood! I don't *care* if they're from your city. I don't *care* if they're the same color as you. I don't *care* if they're on the same journey as you. Nobody owes you nothing! You gotta stay 10 toes down in where you say you wanna be at, where you say you wanna go, what you say you want—put that work in every day and it's gon' come to you. But that entitlement, you better kill that entitlement or that entitlement gon' kill you. And it's just like that!!

10.6.2018

Love Loves Love

Love loves love. You keep talking 'bout you want somebody to show you love, but you ain't showing nobody love! Who you show love to? Think about that. Love loves love! That's the only way you gonna get it, man! Love ain't just something you get outta nowhere—you gotta lead with that. 'C'mon you gotta lead with that. Respect respects respect! Who you respecting? Did you lead with disrespect as soon as you met 'em? And gave it to that 'cause they a human being? Did you do that? But naw, you always want someone to respect you. Why should they respect you when you not respecting them?! Love loves love. Respect respects respect. And it's *just... like... that!!*

11.1.2018

Look at What You Got

Stop looking at what you got, and look at what you *got*! You sitting there looking at, *"Oh, I ain't got this material. I don't live there. I don't have this in my bank account."* That ain't how champions were made. That ain't how everybody you see on Instagram won. They won, because they looked at what they had. You already got it inside of you, that struggle. That let down. Everything. That's what fuels champions! That's what fuels the bosses that you see come down your timeline! That's what fuels the winners! You already got it! Stop looking at what you ain't got and look at what you *got!* Look at what you got! You got it! Everything that Michael Jordan, everything that Lebron had, everything that Oprah had, that struggle—everything they had to go through. That let down, that hurt, that pain, that fear—that's what got them there! They ain't have nothing, but that! And you got it in you. Go out there and get it! And it's just like that!!

11.4.2018

I Prayed for My Enemies

This morning, I prayed for my enemies. But I prayed for my enemies and I asked that they forgive me for thinking about them in the way they think about me. This morning, I prayed for my enemies and I asked God can you please cleanse my heart. Can you please make me a better person. Can you please make sure that I'm not looking at people the way they looking at me, even if they looking at me in a dangerous way. Even if they looking at me in a hateful way. Even if they looking at me in an envious way. God, could you make me better? This morning, I prayed for my enemies. Enemies, please forgive me. Please be understanding, as you would want me to be understanding to you. This morning, I prayed for my enemies. I advise you to pray for your enemies. But don't pray to ask if their heart be cleansed. Pray that your heart be cleansed for the way that you think about them. This morning, I prayed for my enemies. Pray for your enemies.

11.5.2018

Straighten Out Yesterday

Everybody got a yesterday. What we gotta start doing—we gotta straighten out yesterday. We be so focused on going forward and accomplishing our dreams and going to new levels of life, but we ain't straighten out the stuff that was going on yesterday. We ain't clean our backyard out. So now, as we try to grow, as we try to glow and go to the next levels, now this thing will come right to us. And now it'll confront us. Our yesterday will confront us. So if you got people, things, and whatever happened yesterday—problems with people—you gotta go straighten that out. You better straighten it out or they might come and try to straighten you out. That's the reality of it. Or they might come and just stop you from going. They might cross your path and stop right there like, *"No naw—we still got business."* So if it's family, friends, associates, go out there and straighten it out. Communication is everything, so you know, sometimes you just gotta have one conversation and you'll realize it really wasn't as big as it is. And you'll realize that somebody came in between y'all and it wasn't really real what y'all were going through. And it's just like that!

11.6.2018

Push Through!

Everything you want, you got in you! You can do it! Push through! Don't let nobody tell you nothing. They told me every day: I'm a two-time felon. I'm a thief. I'm a liar. I'm a cheater. I'm a robber. I'm a violent individual. They told me all that. But, guess what? I'm out here and I'm getting it! I'm getting it! I'm moving around and I'm getting it! You know why? I didn't let words define me. I didn't let people that don't love me, that don't know me define me! I kept going! And I'mma go every day! I'mma be out here putting it down every day! I'mma be in the mud every day! I'm never gon' forget where I come from and what produced me! That's my energy. You must understand! The bottom dictates the top! The roots hold the tree up! You the roots when you at the bottom. Don't never forget that! I don't care what nobody say, you got this shit! Push through! PUSH THROUGH!!